DATE DUE

FEB 18 1981			
MAR 17 1981			
APR 24 1981			
MAY 5 1982			
DEC 28 '84			
MAY 2 '85			
FEB 28			
APR 11 1988			
APR 14 1988			
APR 17 1991			
JY 20 '93			

170 IDEAL   PRINTED IN U.S.A.

TWICE SEVEN WORDS

TWICE SEVEN WORDS

by

AGNES SANFORD

Published by
ARTHUR JAMES LIMITED
THE DRIFT, EVESHAM, WORCS.

First British Edition 1970

© 1970 Agnes Sanford

All British and Commonwealth rights reserved by the Publishers
Arthur James Limited of Evesham, Worcs., England

SBN 85305 179 8

MADE AND PRINTED IN GREAT BRITAIN BY PURNELL AND SONS, LTD.
PAULTON (SOMERSET) AND LONDON

To

FRANCENA HART

this book is affectionately dedicated

MASTER OF THE BEES

TELL it to the bees,
That they may hush the whirring of their wings
    And mourn awhile.
    For he has found his wings,
More subtle and more numinous than theirs,
And he is trying them in realms afar
    Between the earth and heaven.

    But hearken, little bees!
You need not leave your home, for only he,
The master of the house, has gone away.
The Master of the gardens and the fields,
And all the apple trees that fling their boughs
Over the meadows and the hills, remains
    Forever in the earth.

    Part of life is He,
Of every lily shining in the sun,
And every rose whose fragrance fills the air,
And all the little nameless meadow flowers
    Wherein you find your life.

    So do not fly away,
But gather sweetness from the things of earth
    As even He, in all His agony,
Gathered sweetness from the love of earth
    And made it part of heaven.

                       A.S.

FOREWORD

THIS is not a study book, but a book of meditations. It is meant to speak not so much to the conscious mind as to that inner intelligence that the Bible calls the heart. It should therefore be read slowly, one chapter a day. Since this is not my usual way of communicating, I have woven bits of poetry into these pages, since poetry is a language of the heart.

My own introductory poem concerns a quaint bit of folk-lore suggested by a book by Beverley Nichols. If the master of a house dies, and if he is a keeper of bees, one must go and knock on the hive and tell the bees that their master has departed this life, for if this is not properly announced to them, so declares this ancient bit of fancy, the bees will fly away.

But what have bees to do with Jesus Christ? And what have the trees and flowers and the little earth upon which we live to do with the words of our Lord from the cross, and with His redemptive work upon the cross, and with the mystery of His resurrected life?

Read, and listen from the heart, and you will understand.

CONTENTS

CONTENTS

PART I

SEVEN WORDS FROM THE CROSS

1

FATHER, FORGIVE THEM
Luke 23: 34

NEVER again upraise your leafy heads,
Oh, brother trees, nor flutter in the wind
And sing with joy that all the flying birds
Alight upon your branches. Dance no more,
Oh shining leaves, with rapture in the sun,
Nor let the gentle moonlight give you peace.
For if for Adam's sake the earth was cursed,
Then how much more the trees, when on a tree
The Son of God was hanged until His death?

What was that He said? "Father, forgive.
They know not what they do." Trees did not know
That men would make of wood a cross to kill
The Son of God. But hark! He said, "Forgive,
Take away the guilt from man and earth,
And all the things that live upon the earth."
So lift your heads again, oh brother trees,
And all the butterflies will come to you
With gentle wings of comfort and of joy!

Lift your branches to the singing birds
That fly to you in rapture! Shout aloud
With every passing wind that love has come,

And chosen wood for honour and for praise!
That looking far along the passing years
You see the churches raise a cross on high,
Because it raised on high the loving One
Who took away the ancient sin of man
By pouring out His blood upon a cross!

✠

IN ALL HIS AGONY Jesus took time to forgive those Roman soldiers who were nailing Him to the cross. He *had* to forgive them, or the power of the redemption prayer that included the giving of His life would have been lost.

Prayer is not merely saying words with the lips, nor even in the mind. Effective prayer is the merging of the living human energy in our spirits with the sunburst, the holocaust, the radiance, or the inferno of the ineffable creative light of the creator. The power behind this creative light or energy is the passionate surge of an emotion that we call love: the love that brings forth life. This love can have as its darker component a terrible resistance to evil such as Jesus showed when He cried out against the hypocrisy of the scribes and Pharisees, their words of piety and their acts of cruelty. But this holy zeal for righteousness and intolerance of evil cannot spring from personal hurt or it becomes involved with the slow, dull decay of resentment that more quickly than any other poison separates the soul from God and prevents the effectiveness of prayer.

During the season that we rightly call "Passion week", having no other words great and mysterious enough to describe the work of our Redeemer, Jesus was voluntarily taking into Himself the hate and resentment of all of us so that He could purge us of sin and fill us with His love. He could not, therefore, permit any shadow of personal resentment to stand in the way of this redeeming work, so He

14

cleared the channel of His own soul by forgiving His persecutors.

In doing this He asked God to forgive them. Just as we in His name can pray to the Father, so Jesus asked the Father Himself to re-create them by His power, and this re-creation, this change, began in them at that time. One of the soldiers cried aloud, after death and darkness had descended upon that awful hill, "Surely this was the Son of God!" Even His disciples did not cry out His divinity with such a strong voice as this. Surely the soldier was testifying to the work that the forgiveness of God had already done in him. This, the transformation of personality by the entering in of the love of God, is true forgiveness. This is the love-power that in spite of all evil shall someday awaken men to the knowledge of their royal inheritance.

If forgiving people means merely smiling upon them with smug, false kindness and saying, "I once resented you, but now I forgive you," then let us have none of it, for it would be merely exalting one's own ego by a false statement of forgiveness, and thus inflicting upon the other person a second hurt. Forgiveness that learns to love the other person though he is unlovable comes nearer to the mark of the high tide of the love of Christ.

There is, however, a power of forgiveness that can in fact change the other person and make him lovable, and it is based on two essentials: first, on willingness to suffer for the sake of achieving this power in prayer, and second, on the faith to believe that this prayer will be effective.

There are those who voluntarily undertake a life of hardship, giving up the comfort of wife or husband, the joys of children, the pride of ownership, and even the privilege of directing their own lives. If these devoted monks and nuns, these religious, undertake this vocation for the sake of honouring our Lord, I am sure that their power in prayer is great. The power of the enemy gathers itself against them, however, and the world rolls on in the darkness of hate and agony. Here and there, true, this darkness is lifted by the holy atmosphere shining from those who live a life of prayer; and who can measure the benefits of these bits of light in the darkness? If it had not been for them the world might have destroyed itself before now, but plainly they are not enough, for the earth trembles on the brink of tragedy, and men's hearts fail them for fear.

There are ministers called into God's service and willing to endure all hardship that they may testify to His redeeming love. But how hard it is for them to love each other as Jesus loved us, forgiving all the wounds to sensitive hearts torn by the neglect, jealousy and callousness of vestries, congregations and brother ministers! And there are the lesser Christians, all of us who love our Lord and yet all too often criticize and despise our neighbours, or harbour deep hate caused by the wounds of the past.

Every jealousy, every resentment, of nun against nun, of minister against vestryman, of Christian against Christian, puts one stone in the channel of God's love towards us. Let us but remove these stones, and the rush of His love will cover the earth as the waters cover the sea.

God's love, remember, is not merely a pleasant emotion, the falling-in-love feeling that the Greeks called "eros". Eros may be woven into the bundle of divine love as it is woven into the marriage relationship, wherein love assumes the responsibility of children who must also be loved and cherished and protected from any infringement of love through quarrelling, bickering, and, worst of all, divorce.

Eros can also be led astray and used by Satan to break hearts and marriages, and to ruin the lives of little children. God's love, "agape", cannot be so used. It sees no evil; it desires not its own; it endures all things—and still forgives. And it is a power greater than life and greater than death, and it shall one day overcome the world if only we who are His disciples fling ourselves body and soul into its mighty rush of creative energy. For the power of this love is greater than all the power of violence, and it can without the dropping of one bomb defeat the enemies who would use violence and war.

How do I know? Because it happens! Time and again a city, for instance, has been threatened with violence, and that threat has passed over and gone away, like clouds black with storm that shift and lighten and blow away in peace. The reason, unknown to the world, lay in a little group of those who pray in the invincible power of the love of God that violence shall pass over. Thus the city is protected by the very life of the Lamb which Jesus shed for us when in the midst of great agony He cried out, "Father, forgive them; for they know not what they do."

PRAYER

LET US HOLD up into Thy love now, oh God, one person who has hurt and frightened us and disturbed our peace. Remembering Jesus, let us say, "Father, forgive him for he knows not what he does."

In the name of Jesus Christ, send Thy love into him and heal those wounds in his own heart that cause him to wound others. Comfort him of old sorrows. Melt down in him by love the crust of evil that hides his true nature, for he was born in Thine image and likeness, oh God, and within him there abides a bit of that very light that Jesus Christ brought into the world. Let that hidden light of Jesus, that fragment of the real being of the redeemer, be set free in him now through our forgiving love, and let him be changed into

17

the real self, redeemed and transformed by love, which we now see in our minds by faith.

As we thus remove one stone from the channel of Thy love to us, oh God, let us dare to imagine the creative power of forgiveness sweeping over men and nations and bringing in Thy kingdom upon earth, Amen.

2

TO-DAY SHALT THOU BE WITH ME . . .
Luke 23: 43

WHERE is Paradise? Over the hill.
A valley deep and wide and starred with flowers,
And through the midst of it a quiet stream,
Where dragonflies flash needles of blue flame
And shining rushes quiver in the breeze.

Where is Paradise? Over the hill,
And down a path that wanders through the woods
With blooms on every side: mountain pink,
Tinted cups of laurel, snowy plum,
High and wild among the gentle trees
Clothed in the golden green of early spring.
And as you wander blissful down the path
And fill your hands with flowers, something stirs
Within your mind, and suddenly you know
That you have seen those woodlands many a time,
Far away and wistful, like a dream.

What is Paradise? A garden closed
And long forgotten, yet with tiny shoots
Of crocus, daffodil and hyacinth.
You find them hidden under sodden leaves,

And suddenly you think, "I planted these
Many a year ago! They are my own!"

The Father looked upon the woods of heaven,
The pastures and the gardens, and He said,
"Let us make a garden like to this
Upon the earth!" And so the angels came
And planted earth with seeds from Paradise.
And when we reach that nearest of the heavens,
Not as strangers will we come, but led
By Him who went before us we will gaze,
And cry with tears of rapture, "This is mine!
From long ago my soul remembers this!"

JESUS CARRIED OUT His work of redemption even on the
cross. He Himself forgave, as we are also commanded to
forgive in His name, not only those who were crucifying
Him but also the thief on the cross beside Him. That man
had not sinned against Jesus, but against the world and the
laws of the land. He was an enemy of society, but in his last
hours he saw the majesty of Jesus that shone even through
death, and he cried out to Him for mercy.

Jesus helped the thief in the same way that we can help
one sick at heart who asks for help. Jesus did not counsel
with him; there was no time for counselling. He did not
give him good advice. He simply projected into the thief a
current of His own redeeming love, so that the weight of sin
was taken from him and his spirit came back to life. Thus he
was able to be with Jesus in paradise.

What is paradise? It is the first step into the unknown,
where life exists at a different rate of vibration, in many
dimensions, in ways that we cannot understand. There are
two worlds which are yet, in a way, one world. At this present

time we live in both the seen and the unseen. We are two-fold beings, made physically of the dust of the earth as all living creatures are evolved, but made spiritually of the very breath of God.

"But I never thought about our living in two worlds at once," you may say. Probably not, and this could be the reason for the inner restlessness that you continually try to forget. The other one of you, who is spiritual, may be trying to get out of the cage of the flesh, or in some way to express itself through the cramping barriers of the rational mind. Young people particularly feel this restlessness, this deep dissatisfaction with life on this earth. Therefore they try to rise into a consciousness of the spiritual world in dangerous ways such as taking drugs which can destroy the mind and fracture the personality.

There are, however, other ways, simple, straightforward ways, of feeling the love and light of the spiritual world. We can turn to Jesus and ask for His forgiveness, as the thief was really doing when he said, "Lord, remember me when thou comest into thy kingdom." And then our spirits, the locked-up spiritual energies within us, can come to life as did those of the thief. How do I know that his spirit did come to life? Because Jesus promised him that he would be with Him in paradise, and I believe that promise.

Paradise is the threshold of heaven, the first stage of our journey into eternity. I have not seen it except in dreams or flashes of imagining, but I am sure that even now Jesus can say to one who is departing, "To-day shalt thou be with me in paradise."

I once prayed for a little boy suffering with leukaemia. He made for a while an apparent recovery, but then the disease returned in galloping form and he was back in the hospital. The doctors told his parents that he would live for about six weeks, with much suffering. He did not, however, suffer any pain whatsoever, and at the end of the first week as his mother sat by his bed, he said to her, "Mother, I see Jesus, and He's beckoning to me. Is it all right if I go with Him now?"

The mother very wisely said, "Yes dear, it's all right if you go with Him now."

And so the child was with Jesus in paradise. I can imagine the little boy holding Jesus' hand and gazing about with wonder and delight. I can imagine all the beautiful things through which God speaks to us—flowers and trees, flowing waters and green pastures—existing there in a different form, more vibrant, more full of life, perhaps fluid and changing, perhaps shining with immortality. As the little boy would follow Jesus, as he would in some fashion grow up and attain maturity in heaven—for so I believe we do—he would indeed go from strength to strength, and from stage to stage.

In the Bible we are told of spiritual beings of tremendous power and glory—angels, archangels, cherubim, seraphim. We are told of strange, mysterious creatures described symbolically: the four and twenty elders, the four and twenty beasts. We are told of the great white throne. The dying thief would not be expected on his very first day to see all these wondrous and glorious things. It would be terrifying and incomprehensible to him if he did. So I do not know how much he was able to see at the beginning, but this I know: he was with Jesus in paradise.

The word used for paradise in the Bible is the same word that is sometimes translated hades. It does not mean hell any more than it means the heaven of heavens. It means simply the place of the departed, an ante-room, a waiting room. Indeed the old word purgatory may not be wrong, for surely the soul needs time to be cleansed of the heavy vibrations of earth, to be changed into the kind of being who can live forever, and who would want to live forever.

When faced by great mysteries I sometimes just ask the

Lord to speak, and tell me as much as He thinks I can understand, and then I listen. As I listened this morning these words came to me, entering of course through the veil of my own mind which does not claim to be infallible.

"I am Lord of all," said the Lord, "of the dead and of the living, for in my sight all live. Consciousness is not destroyed by the death of the body. Consciousness—that is, the life of the soul—remains, and perceives and experiences immortality in so far as it is prepared to do so. The thief upon the cross might have first felt heaven only as a burning anguish if he had not already opened his eyes to it by perceiving it in me upon the cross.

"The glories of heaven could have been all around the thief and yet appear to him only as darkness, just as the sun can shine all around a blind man and yet remain unseen by him. The thief had been spiritually blind all his life. The breath of God, though born within him, was sealed off from his conscious mind, and every time he broke my laws the veil between spirit and mind grew thicker and thicker. His mind was so filled with evil and cruelty that he could not see goodness and love until he saw them in me. Then he cried out for mercy, and his memories were healed so that he could be with me in paradise, seeing with my eyes and living in my love.

"To you also, since you are Christians called by my name, is given the mysterious power to pray for the healing of the memories, not only of those who live upon this earth but of those who have gone on into the next world. When you forgive someone who has been chained to you in this life by anger and has now departed, that forgiveness will reach him even in the next world and set him free.

"How far back can this forgiveness go? How many of the chains that you carry were put upon you by your ancestors, by the sins of the Church throughout the ages, by the

23

cruelties of the world throughout the ages? How far back can your forgiveness go?"

✠

PRAYER

OH LOVING and wonderful Lord Jesus, you have asked questions that we cannot answer. But now as we stand at the foot of your cross we meditate upon the wonder of your love, that even in the anguish of dying you still were able to say to the thief, "To-day shalt thou be with me in paradise."

Open now new doors in our minds, oh Lord! Go through us as far as your love can go, forgiving and setting free! And in your name we say, "Father, forgive," for the sins of those who have not known you. Let your forgiveness rush like the flow of mighty power into all churches that call upon your name but do not do your works, shaking them into new awareness and new faith. Remove from us the punishment that we as a people do most justly deserve. And lift us up, oh Lord, the first step into heaven, so that while we are here in the flesh our souls may even now be with you in paradise, Amen.

3

WHY HAST THOU FORSAKEN ME?
Mark 15: 34

Out of the night—shattering the dark
That made a night of noonday, as the light
Of Christmas evening made the midnight day—
Out of the blackest anguish ever known,
And yet not known, for who could bear the weight
Of knowledge such as this—the cry went forth,
Between the earth and unresponding heaven,
While angels hid their faces in their wings.
He spoke for all of us. He cried aloud
The cry of every man, that He might give
To every man the joy of sins forgiven.
Oh Son of God, who yet was every man,
Out of the travail of your deepest woe,
Children of light were born—the sons of God!

How often have we said these very words, crying to God
out of the depth of our great need! Yet He has not forsaken
us any more than the sun has forsaken the solar system when
its light is hidden behind clouds. It is our own sins of wrong-
doing, of fear and of despair that have hidden God from
the eyes of our souls.

Jesus, however, was the very Son of God, and walked always in God's light. He had no sins. He was tempted, as all men are tempted, but He resisted temptation always and was triumphant over it. Why then did He think God had forsaken Him?

So we would have thought if we had been upon that cross. He had become us. He had so completely immersed himself in the sins of the world that He had become sin for us. This was at once His darkest and His most triumphant moment for He had achieved His objective; He had become man. He was all the way down. It was not His own sins that had "got Him down", as we so truly say. It was *our* sins, but He was there, in the very depth of the sins of mankind. Therefore He can reach us when we are in the depths, caught under the driftwood of aimless living and smothering under the mud-slides of evil thinking. We cannot get out by ourselves. We are entangled in aimless and futile struggling from which we see no escape. We are thick and muddy in our thinking, unable to control sluggish thought patterns of nameless uneasiness. We are chained beneath the depths of life; we are imprisoned. Jesus could not possibly find us and set us free save that He Himself plumbed the depths, when even the face of God was hidden from His sight, when He felt Himself forsaken even as we feel ourselves forsaken.

Because Jesus entered into the depths a part of Him is forever there. "If I make my bed in hell, behold, thou art there," wrote David (Psalm 139: 8). Forever He has access to those depths. Therefore He comes when we call upon Him, gently untangles us from the driftwood, digs us out of the mud that has well-nigh covered us, and bears us up out of the depths into the sunlight of God's love.

Jesus gave His life to do this, going beyond what a life-saver might do in risking his life to rescue a drowning man. If we were caught in the depths and someone entered those depths to save us, would we not make every effort to co-operate with him? Would we refuse his help? Would we say that it was too much trouble to try to hold on to him and clamber out?

What then shall be our reasonable response to Jesus' death on the cross? Repentance! Change! We must turn round and go in the opposite direction! Repentance involves sorrow. Certain people say, *"Our* sins placed Him upon the cross," and it is true that since we are part of the great mass of humanity our own personal sins did have a part in placing Jesus on the cross. It is meet and right that we should consider this, that we should look into ourselves and ask the Holy Spirit to reveal to us in a more real and stark fashion what these sins may be, so that we may correct them, and what these failures to send forth power may be, so that we may indeed send it forth in His name.

Just to be sorry for our sins is not the actual accomplishment of repentance; it is merely the first step toward it. Repentance is seeing where we have gone wrong and then turning round and going in the right direction. True, we do need to see where we have taken a wrong turn, just as a driver needs to see that he has taken a wrong turning on the route he wanted to take. It would do a driver no good, however, just to sit there and mourn forever at his mistake. He would be wise to waste as little time as possible in blaming himself for his error, and immediately turn round and seek the right road. He must know and believe that there is a right way. If he did not know this, then he would indeed be lost! So we should know and believe that through the work of our Redeemer there is established for us a right way. We should believe that He has the power and the love to turn us about and start our footsteps on the path of peace. Knowing this, we should waste no time mourning about the past, but should look toward the future, and seek and find the right way.

Some people say, "Jesus died for me, and if I were the

only person living upon the face of the earth, He still would have died for me." That may or may not be true. We have no way of knowing whether or not He would have given His life for one person, but I rather hope not, as it would seem a great waste of His energy. Saying this, however, is an attempt to arouse people to the one essential, which is repentance, and the only true repentance must lead to a new and stronger life. If we do not truly believe that the redemption of Jesus Christ can dig us out of the depths of our sins, we make His life-saving effort of no avail.

Do we in fact believe that we can develop out of being miserable sinners into the glory of becoming the sons of God? If we look no further than the cross we cannot become the sons of God. The cross prepares the way by emptying the deep mind of its burdens of grief and pain and sin. The cross makes the way plain, beating through the wilderness of our memories a pathway for our God. But the cross does not fill the empty spaces left by our own troubles and griefs. The holy drama of our Lord Jesus Christ, God dwelling in man on earth, is not completed unless we go on from the cross and attain to the indwelling and infilling of His Holy Spirit, because only by the power of the Holy Spirit can our repentance be crowned with victory.

Therefore as we kneel before Him, grieving indeed and truly that our sins had a part in placing Him upon the cross, let us begin now to have a part in comforting Him, making Him happy, fulfilling the purpose for which He died upon the cross. If it is true that though we live two thousand years later our sins have their part in placing Him upon the cross, then it is equally true that our obedience and our victories in power, our living a new life, our doing His works even as He said we should do them, can have a part now in comforting Him.

✠

PRAYER

OH LORD, show us our sins that we may know where we have failed you. With a mighty forging you welded for us the redeeming power of your love, with which we were to go forth and bring light into the darkness of this world: wholeness to the sick and broken in heart, comfort to the comfortless, hope of everlasting life to those lost in darkness. We have tried to do these works, but we have tried with human power only, and the kingdom of heaven has not come. Only by your victory can the power of darkness be overcome. Only by the light of your Holy Spirit can the kingdom of heaven come upon this earth.

So, Lord, forgive us, and even now as we wait before you, pour out upon us through your Holy Spirit the power of your redemptive love so that we can step forth into the world as channels of that love, helping you in the great work of bringing in your kingdom, Amen.

4

WOMAN, BEHOLD THY SON! BEHOLD THY MOTHER!
John 19: 26, 27

SHE called Him to her once; He would not come.
One flame and only one flared up to heaven
And filled His burning heart—the Father's will.
Men must hear His words before they died,
Or blew their earth to pieces! They must keep
Their Father's orders written in their hearts,
Illumined by His words! Those who heard
Gave life unto His spirit, and received
Life again from Him, more real a life
Than any human mother could bestow,
Even on her son. Yet now at last,
When all His work was done, He turned to her,
And spoke from out His heart before it brake,
"Behold thy son." So the beloved John
Led her away that she might not behold
A death that even angels could not see,
But hid their faces in their shuddering wings,
And shrouded day with darkness, while the blood
Dripped slowly to the ground and filled the earth,
The wounded earth, with all the love of God.

SURELY THIS IS ONE of the most heart-breaking incidents in the whole story of the cross. Alone among all the women the mother of Jesus had the courage to stand at the foot of the cross and watch that unbearable sight, while alone among all the disciples the beloved disciple John had the courage to stand and watch with her.

Jesus endured the cross, despising the shame, for the glory that was set before Him. One wonders whether or not the mother of Jesus also was able to maintain her faith and to know that there was yet glory set before Him. This had been told her long ago by the angel who announced His coming, and by the prophet Simeon who took Him into his arms in the temple and blessed Him. "Behold," said Simeon, "this child is set for the fall and rising again of many in Israel" (Luke 2: 34). Indeed many in Israel did fall because of Him. They fell because they could not believe that He really was the Messiah. He was not the kind of king that they expected. They looked for a king who would preach a social gospel, reforming society and setting the people free from Rome, and so they could not see the glory of His spiritual kingdom.

The prophet Simeon, however, looked farther. "For the fall and *rising again* of many in Israel," he said. This resurgence of life in the Jewish people has not yet come, and perhaps it cannot come until we who call ourselves Christians learn to show His love to these His brethren.

The prophet Simeon also said to Mary, the mother of Jesus, "Yea, a sword shall pierce through thine own soul also" (Luke 2: 35). As she stood at the foot of the cross, a sword did indeed pierce through her heart. What gave her then the courage to endure? It must have been that she remembered the glory that was set before Him which was still to be revealed. She did not lose faith nor give up hope, but even so, the anguish of it was beyond anything that we can imagine.

As far as we know, Mary was the only one of His family who stood by Jesus in this hour, either literally by the cross or spiritually and mentally believing in Him. Jesus could not stay in Nazareth, His home. He could do no mighty works there because of the people's unbelief. Therefore among the many griefs that overwhelmed this woman, the mother of Jesus, there might have been another, smaller but real. Where should she go? Whither could she flee? Those of her own home in rejecting Jesus surely would reject her also, so if they did not openly reject her, how could she live among them when their faith in Him was so utterly lacking? There was no one who understood—no one. It would seem obvious that Joseph, her husband, had passed away by then, because from the time when Jesus was twelve years old Joseph is not mentioned in the gospels, great and good man though he was.

Jesus, even in the midst of His anguish, seeing His mother, He knew her great need of someone to understand, love and comfort her even as He understood and loved her. True, He refused to be tied to her apron-strings, as we can see from the time when His mother and His brothers, so we are told, came when He was teaching in the midst of a crowd and called to Him. Perhaps they thought, "He has really gone off the deep end. What sort of trouble is He getting into? We must persuade Him to come home." But He would not heed them. "Who is my mother? and who are my brethren?" He said (Matt. 12: 48). Thus, as every person must do on reaching maturity, Jesus cut the spiritual umbilical cord that would have bound Him to His mother, but He never cut the bond of love. This we know because of His words, "Behold thy son." And from that moment John took her into his own home.

We rejoice that Jesus, even in the midst of all His anguish, did not lose touch with the physical needs of this earth, the need of His mother for comfort and shelter, for a home with someone who understood. And we rejoice that now that He has risen into the heavens, and His glory that was with Him from the beginning has returned to Him, He still does not lose touch with this human earth. He is still aware of our physical needs—the need of a home, the need of love, the need of someone to understand, to cherish and to comfort.

PRAYER

OH WONDERFUL Saviour, we give thanks that it is Thy desire not only to endue us with power so that we may show forth Thy glory to the world, but also to cherish us and tenderly to care for us. We give thanks that we can trust Thee to provide for us a home and love, and we pray that Thy love may flow forth through us in tenderness and concern to others who need a home, and love, and someone to cherish them.

We rejoice that Thy love encompasses even the little needs of our everyday lives. So now, oh Lord, we turn from great things to small things and we hold up before Thee whatever needs are in our lives and in the lives of our friends: needs of shelter, of a home, of the money to keep or to maintain that home, of someone to love, of someone to understand. We pray with faith that Thy love will never forget us, that Thy promises will be fulfilled, and that our every need will be met. In Jesus' name, Amen.

5

I THIRST
John 19: 28

Why do you tremble so in the still wind,
The hardly-breathing breath of the far place
    That you can never see?

"Listen!" So the lilies seem to say.
"What is this we hear?" Only a man
Crying aloud, "I thirst." Only a God
Dying and far away. "We see no man,
But every flower in the garden hears.
The iris droops its purple head and dies.
The flaming poppies pale and turn to dust.
The rose drops all her petals to the ground.
Even the pansy hides its kitten face
    And looks at life no more.
There is no life. Nothing exists but death,
And in the night the heavens moaning low,
    While all the stars are hid."

Something quivers down the garden path.
A light—a tongue of fire—a rippling wind?
Something whispers deep within the earth,
"There is no death, only the pulse of life
That surges in and surges out again.

And from the blood of Him who dies athirst
There rushes in a new and deeper life—
    The very life of God."

SUCH A SIMPLE CRY to split the midday night on Calvary!
Darkness was gathering round Him as darkness often comes
upon a man in dying, the light fading from his eyes as his
soul prepares to leave the body and go on into a greater
light. But this man was also God, the creator of all light and
life. Thus in the time of His departing, while His whole
body was tortured by thirst, the shadows deepened. At
first men knew not the cause of the darkness, thinking—
if they thought at all—that thunder was arising out of the
sea. And so it was.

Out of this enfolding dark He cried, "I thirst!" A soldier—
one of those whom He had asked the Father to forgive—held
up to Him on a reed a sponge soaked in vinegar mingled with
gall. This same drink had been offered Him earlier in the
trial (Matt. 27: 34), but when He tasted of it He would not
drink it. It was probably a pain-killer, such as morphine.
Why then would He not accept it? Is there any value *per
se* simply in suffering? If so, why was Jesus never sick? Why
did He never lie down and have a migraine headache or a
nervous breakdown? Why, moreover, did He never say to
anyone who came to Him for healing, "No, it will make you
more holy to suffer pain?" He never did that, not once. Never
in any instance did He intimate that the mere fact of
suffering pain could possibly be according to God's will. If
this had been so, then He would have been in disobedience
to God as He went about healing the sick and relieving those
who suffered. One of the worst heresies ever taught is that
Jesus suffered on the cross to show men how to suffer bravely,
because it is good to endure pain.

Many dark hours later, Jesus asked for the drink that He had earlier refused. St. John, who stood by Him for the entire time of His dying until Jesus Himself sent him away, gives us the reason for this. He says, "Jesus knowing that all things were now accomplished... saith, I thirst" (John 19:28).

He knew that His work was drawing to a close. He had gathered into Himself all the dregs of man's sin, and the last bits of its fleeing darkness were tearing their way through His soul. It was now permissible that He accept a little bit of comfort for His agony. Therefore He said, "I thirst."

More than any other word from the cross, this makes clear to us that His death was not a tragedy but a redemption, not a failure but the triumphant conclusion of the greatest act of history: God dying as man, in full awareness of all the sin and suffering of mankind, so that man could live in God's righteousness and joy and glorious health, and then, in dying, open his eyes to a new-old world of eternal glory.

Oh wonder of redemptive love! With every breath Jesus drew into Himself man's sin and felt the pain of it, so that in every breath He could create for man the eternal torrent of God's love able to flow back through time and on through time, washing away all the filth of sin and taking away even the heavy stones of grief. This is what He did in that incomparable act of redemption. His death was not merely the unfortunate death of a martyr, like that of Socrates or Stephen or Joan of Arc. His death was the merging of acquired death into eternal life for all who accepted Him. It was the reversal of the death-trend of mankind, swinging it into power to go through life to Life, as Enoch and Elijah went, the very body redeemed and not decayed.

Jesus did this in full awareness, refusing until very near the end the pain-killing vinegar mixed with gall, not because He preferred to suffer but because He needed complete clarity of mind to accomplish His work of redemption. The

36

physical suffering was secondary to the "glory that was set before Him". A mountain climber may suffer intensely as he reaches a high peak. Every breath is agony, every step excruciating pain. Why does he go on? To reach the summit, naturally. If he could reach it without pain that would be wonderful, but he cannot, and therefore he endures the pain. An athlete may suffer intense agony as he races toward his goal. Why does he continue? Is it because he values suffering for its own sake? No! It is to win the race.

Jesus was an athlete of the spirit, contending for a tremendous prize—the redemption of mankind. His final race began in the garden of Gethsemane when He faced the total power of evil in the world to turn it into good. We certainly cannot understand the work of the redemption. We can think of it only in metaphors, inadequate symbols. We might say that He took into Himself a current of evil, like a current of electricity, and within Himself changed its rate of vibration, so that what came in as evil and hate went forth as goodness and love.

Jesus told us to take up the cross and follow Him. How can we do so? Plainly not by being sick. That is too small and limited a suffering to be likened to His cross. Rather, we should strive for His sake to overcome both illness and any sins that may have brought it upon us. We cannot follow Jesus merely by having arthritis, for instance, and being a great sufferer. The pious sigh, "Jesus suffered, and I must suffer too," is a travesty of holiness, and makes His redemptive suffering of no avail. Jesus did not go by that road. He did not have arthritis or colitis or cancer, or any of the body-withering and soul-withering diseases that we tend to bring upon ourselves.

A friend of mine, on recovering from a "fatal" disease, wrote to me thus: "I am very thankful to be healed of the selfish suffering of illness so that I can suffer more effectually in His service."

Yes, there are ways of following Him, and they are not easy. We can follow Him by obeying Him, and striving to learn the power of faith and how to do His works (John 14: 12). We can endure the hardness of keeping His rules of life, that rigorous list of training exercises in the life of the spirit that Jesus outlined in the Sermon on the Mount (Matt. 5–7), and that God prefigured through Moses in the ten commandments (Ex. 20: 1–17). We can make the supreme sacrifice of loving one another as He loved us, according to His commandment. We can carry His love to far places, and to those who live in darkness and in the shadow of death. We can carry it also to near places and the little people among whom we live and work. Thus, truly following Jesus, we can channel to all mankind the work of redemption that He accomplished for us on the cross.

Thus—and only thus—will His divine thirst for the souls of men at last be assuaged. Thus—and only thus—will His heart, broken for us, be fully comforted.

PRAYER

FORGIVE US, LORD, that as we read these words our spirits faint and falter, not daring to believe. Help us each to know that Jesus died enduring to the end so that we might drink of the water of life that comes from Him and ever live!

True, we may not in this generation see the overcoming of death. We may not see it in this century or in this millennium, not until the age of the ages is past and time is melted into Time. But may our awareness grow, so that the power grows within us. May the waves of eternity beat upon us more and more strongly until as we wade into death we find that we are doing so with joy, as into a shining sea, our minds

open and alert for the very beginning of the new life, needing no vinegar mingled with gall but only the balm of Thy
redeeming love, Lord Jesus.

Thus may the final thirst of our departing hours become
a thirst for Thee, and lead directly to Thy throne. And may
our awareness both of life and Life, both of pain and joy,
both of darkness and light, be merged mysteriously into the
channel of Thy redeeming-love, Amen.

6

IT IS FINISHED
John 19: 30

"It is finished." Open then the grave,
And let the groaning earth prepare to take
The One who made the earth. Oh, Abel's blood
That cried aloud to God from out the ground,
You are avenged at last. Oh, ravaged earth,
Blood of our brothers poisoning your breast—
Your clean and fragrant breast, giver of life,
And last and lonely hiding-place of death—
Be comforted at last, for He has come
To pour the cleansing life out of Himself
Into your very depths, that you may live,
Enfolded in the everlasting love
Of Him who brought you forth from nothingness
To be the very kingdom of the Lord.

So a mother might sigh when after long labour her child is born into the world. So a doctor might moan at the end of a six-hour operation as the perspiration stands cold upon his forehead. So a soldier might shout when his troopship upon the high seas turns slowly about and the shadows fall on the stern instead of on the foredeck, and she is headed home because the war is over. This happened at the end of the second world war. Troops upon the high seas beheld the changing shadows on the deck and wondered why the ship should turn right about in the midst of the Pacific Ocean. Then the cry went up, "It is finished! The war is over!"

The voyage of our Redeemer upon the ocean of life was finished. He had turned right about, out of the darkness of humanity and back again slowly, slowly, into the light of God. He was headed home. Once more He saw His Father, and knew that the Father had never forsaken Him. Remembering the black moment when He had cried out, "My God, my God, why hast thou forsaken me?" He saw that moment receding into the shadows of the past, and light shone upon His face as He turned home again.

We can never understand the fullness of this sacrifice, so great that even He lost faith, for the moment, in the Father's love. But let us try to understand it in so far as we can. Let us ask ourselves again, in childish simplicity: "Why did He die for us?"

Was it merely to see how it felt to live and die as a man? Was it merely so that we can know that if we are drowned in sorrow He can comfort us because He also knew sorrow? Was it merely so that He could show us how to forgive? Or merely to drown Himself in the depths of man's sin and thus teach us to die bravely and forgivingly as He died?

No! If our understanding stops at this point, we have missed the final purpose of the redemption.

All the above concepts are true, but they are peripheral. They miss the central point. Yes, it is good to know that Jesus understands all our suffering because He suffered too. It may be consoling if a doctor says, "Yes, I know how miserable you are, for I have been miserable too," but his sympathy is of little use unless he can heal us. A lifeguard dives into deep water to rescue a drowning man, not merely to say, "Oh yes, I know how you feel as you drown."

Jesus chose to enter into the sins of mankind not merely to teach us patiently to endure the results of sin. He became man to take away the dark shadow of a sinful propensity. He came that we may become new creatures in Him. When He enters, the inner darkness is gone; it has been turned into light. Shadows of it may, of course, come upon us again as Satan tries to tempt us, but as the tempter comes he can find no foothold in us, no crack in our armour of light, and the shadows lift again. This is redemption, begun by our Lord in the garden of Gethsemane, completed on the cross and perfected within us through the work of the sanctifier, the Holy Spirit.

Jesus did not die so that we could merely copy His example and die bravely. Oh travesty of truth! Oh dullness beyond belief, that we should try to reduce His glorious act to a mere "way-showing", as if to say, "Look, this is the way to die!" Jesus died for us so that some far day we could by His power overcome death and go from life to Life without passing through those doors.

It had taken all the strength He had to do this work, and at the very end of it He cried out, with what relief we cannot even begin to imagine, "It is finished!" This was a cry of triumph, for now our Lord knew that the work that He was doing was complete. The very last dregs of the misery of mankind had entered into Him. The very last wickedness of mankind had pierced through His soul and out again into the Father's care. The terrible shadow of being separated from God the Father had passed away. It was done! It was finished! The child was born! The new humanity was at this time potentially given birth.

True, it remains for us to complete this work of redemption, but His part of it was completed. Potentially, that in us which is evil was put to death on the cross. If we are willing and brave enough to claim that deliverance, then we have through the cross the power to overcome all that was once evil and turn it into good. Every grievous fault within us can be turned into a glorious virtue because He died for us. A bad temper can be turned into fiery zeal for His name's sake. Selfishness can be turned into a spontaneous flow of unselfish love. Lust or misdirected love can be transformed into a passion of divine love—the love that goes forth to seek and to save those that are lost, the divine compassion of Christ that flows to anyone needing that love, man, woman, or child, seeking not to possess but only to liberate—the divine, releasing love of God.

Jesus said, "It is finished." His part of the redemption was done. It remains for us to enter into this redemption, because He gave us free will and therefore He will not impose anything upon us. His regenerative power has been created and set free for us to seek and to use. The power of the kingdom of heaven, the power of the Holy Spirit, was made possible for us through the redemption, and we will go on, praise God, to the receiving of this power.

PRAYER

LORD, help us to finish our work upon earth even as you finished the task set before you: the redemption of mankind. Help us to become a new species—the sons of God, the children of the eternal for whom the whole creation waits— that we may make this still-travailing earth into the kingdom of heaven.

Use our prayers in ways mysterious and unseen, even down through ages far ahead, even back through dark mysteries of time, to lighten the darkness, rebuild the city of God, and bring it to live upon the earth, Amen.

7

INTO THY HANDS . . .
Luke 23: 46

YOUR spirit lived before the earth was born!
　Darkness fled away before the sight
Of terrifying glory on the morn
　When you, the Word of God, created light.

What binding pain to live upon the earth
　And feel the sins of men, and hear their cry!
But now your finished work has given birth
　To all the sons of God—and you may die.

Oh grant me, Lord, my length of days to know,
　That when the time has come to turn my face
Up to the skies, and stretch my spirit's wings,
　I'll know my work is finished, and will go
With eager longing to that heavenly place,
　Where evermore the whole creation sings!

IT WAS FINISHED. All that He came to do for humanity had
been completed. Therefore Jesus could see the Father again.
God had not forsaken Him. The light returned to Him.
The glory returned to Him. And so He commanded His own

spirit to leave Him, saying, "Father, into thy hands I commend my spirit."

What a wonderful thing it would be if, when our time comes to leave the earth, we also should be able to go with rejoicing, to will our departure, to say these same words which Jesus said! It amazes me that we who are Christians, named with the name of Christ, are so afraid of death, so uncertain about our departure into the next world that we do not even want to speak about it. To hear us talk, one would think that there is no such thing as death. Of course, when the kingdom comes then there shall indeed be no more death. But the kingdom has not yet come in its fullness, and in this day and generation we may as well face the fact that death does exist. Indeed, who would want to live forever on this earth and in this present type of body!

It is strange to me that Christian people do not make it a practice to think and talk about death and immortality, imagining the glories of heaven in order to prepare for the eternal life. It would be very foolish of me to go on a mission without making any preparations—deciding what I should wear, what I should take with me, where I shall go, and what I shall do. How much more foolish to go into the next life without preparation, without any prayers, without any questioning of the Lord: "What do you want me to do there? Where am I to go?"

Of course we are not allowed to see all the mysteries of the eternal life in which our souls already live. It is too great for us; we cannot comprehend it. But there are glimpses of heaven that we can see, as did St. Paul and St. John and many another in the Bible. These glimpses may be symbolic or they may be literal. They may be trying to tell us through pictures or through words about things that cannot really be seen in pictures or understood through words; but they mean something to our souls nevertheless.

Therefore let us know that we need not be afraid of death.

45

There is, of course, the human tendency to fear, but let us seek to rise above it, not by saying, "I am not afraid," for that does not go deep enough. Let us seek to overcome the fear of death by imagining, by meditating at times, upon the other life which is not seen with the eyes, the life of the heavenly kingdom. Then when the time does come for us to go, and when we know that the time is drawing nigh, we need not fight to stay upon this earth, but can say with Jesus, "Father, into thy hands I commend my spirit," and go forth willingly and with joy. When that time comes for our loved ones, let us not hold them upon this earth, falsely clinging merely to the physical body, but let us be able and willing to say, as did the mother in the story I told in the second meditation, "Yes dear, it's all right if you go with Him now."

There is a difference, however, between our departure into heaven and that of our Lord. He apparently took a detour that, so far as we know, we do not take. So let us now turn our meditation to the very puzzling question: where was Jesus Himself during those three days when His body was in the tomb? We know that when the body dies the spirit, or consciousness, is no longer in it. One has only to see a corpse to know that. Christian people say that the spirit of a departed loved one has "gone to heaven", but Jesus had not gone to heaven, as He plainly told Mary Magdalene in the garden on Easter morning: "Touch me not; for I am not yet ascended to my Father" (John 20:17). During those three days then He was not in the high heavens among the thundering praise of the angels and archangels, nor was He upon earth in the glimmering future of the bringing forth of the sons of God.

Then where was His spirit, His consciousness, during those three days? Peter knew (1 Pet. 3: 19–20), and we have accepted his knowledge and woven it into our Apostles' Creed. How did Peter know? Let us imagine. Let us make

ourselves a little play about Peter, that blundering fellow full
of an insatiable curiosity.

Peter: Yes, but where were you? You weren't in the body,
for it was dead.

Jesus: No, I was not in the body. Often even in sleep one is
not quite in the body. One goes afar in dreams; one
prays for the seen and for the unseen.

Peter: But you were not asleep. You were dead. *Where did
you go?*

Jesus: Back in time, to find my lost children.

Peter: I don't understand. How far back in time?

Jesus: Remember Noah, and all those who died by drowning and by sudden death?

Peter: Why did you not warn them, as you warned
Noah?

Jesus: I did, but they did not hear me. So while my body
was in the tomb I entered into death even as I
entered into life upon this planet, and so I found
them, far on the other side of death.

PRAYER

OH SON OF GOD, long departed from death into life, what
did you tell them? What could you possibly have told them
except the word of eternal love that is the very nature of
God? And could that love melt down their earthly crust,
and break through their barriers of corruption, and bring
them a seed of hope from which in the far reaches of eternity
new life could grow?

I cannot hear your answer, Lord, yet I feel it in my
heart as a sense of hope and comfort. I can trust you not
only for my loved ones here, but also for my loved ones
who departed this earth seeing you but dimly from afar.

Some of them may be lost in time, but you are a part of all time, and through all time you can move and you can love. Will you look for them, Lord Jesus, those whom I hold up to you in love? And when you find them, will you stretch forth your hand to them and call them home? Amen.

PART II

SEVEN WORDS AFTER THE CROSS

8

WHOM SEEKEST THOU?
John 20: 15

HE STOOD before her and she knew Him not.
Torn with the frantic fantasy of hope,
And anguished with the shattering distress
Of torture and of death and of the tomb,
She could not see the glory in His face—
His form still shimmering in heaven's light,
Quivering as in the summer's heat
The very mountains quiver in the light.
Then He called her name—and so she knew.
Oh call us by our names, most holy One,
That we may see you, as this very day
You stand before us, and we know you not.

"WHOM SEEKEST THOU?" So Jesus asked Mary Magdalene
when He saw her weeping in the garden. She was seeking
Jesus Himself beyond His open tomb, but she looked upon
Him and did not know Him.

No wonder she did not know Him. She was looking for a
dead body, and He was a living person. Sometimes when we
seek Him and do not know Him the reason may be that we
are looking for a dead body. We are looking for an historical

character, whom we vaguely conceive to be in some mysterious way existing in the heavens, but whom we do not expect to see even with the eyes of faith as a person who lives and moves upon this earth.

How shall we see Him? In the way that we "see" the wind, perhaps. We perceive things move when the wind passes by, and we believe that it is the wind that causes them to move. We can see Jesus, a living Jesus, if we see things move when He passes by. When the sick are healed as they pray to Him, when the lost are found, when those dead in soul are resurrected, then we see a living Jesus.

Mary Magdalene had gone early to the sepulchre, while it was yet dark. She knew that a great stone had been rolled upon that sepulchre, and that the seal of the holy Roman empire was on that stone. I do not know if she went merely to be near the corpse that had once contained the spirit of Jesus Christ, or if she went because of an instinctive feeling, a guiding even though she did not recognize it. But there she stood before the sun rose. And the stone was no longer blocking the door of the sepulchre!

A great angel had come and rolled away the stone, and we read that at sight of him the keepers shook with fear and became as dead men. (I wonder if they went back and fell to the ground as the soldiers did in the garden of Gethsemane, stunned, temporarily rendered unconscious by God's power.) The stone was rolled away, not to let Jesus out, for His resurrected body could move through stone or wood or anything, but to let the disciples enter and see that He was no longer there.

Beholding the empty tomb, Mary Magdalene said, weeping, "They have taken away my Lord and I know not where they have laid Him" (John 20: 13). When the disciples heard, John ran to the sepulchre and saw the linen clothes lying, and yet he did not go in. Then Simon Peter came, and he saw the linen clothes lying, and the napkin that was about His head not lying with the linen clothes but wrapped together in a place by itself.

The linen clothes were long pieces of cloth that were wrapped around the corpse to embalm it with spices and herbs. The one that had been wrapped around the head was separate from those round the body. The disciples saw these clothes still lying in neat folds, not torn apart and scattered on the ground, nor in any way rumpled or disturbed. What had happened to that body? How and in what manner did our Lord Jesus raise that body from the dead, as He promised that He would do?

We cannot completely understand this mystery, but we can meditate upon it and wonder. Wondering opens the soul, and as we continue to hold the mind open by wondering, we shall some day understand mysteries that even the disciples did not grasp.

So then, let us contemplate—let us wonder. What happened to the body of Jesus? I imagine something like this: that the living spirit of our Lord, after His mysterious journey into the gates of hell, came again into the cave and poured new spiritual energy into that body. Then I imagine that the living spirit of Jesus re-entered that body, and by His transcendent power changed every cell into a different kind of cell, a new order of being. Thus He created a body that was able to manifest itself in solid flesh, and that was also able to transfer its energy into the spiritual realm and become pure spirit, passing through any kind of matter, and disappearing.

Then I imagine that body rising out of the grave clothes and gradually forming itself into a body that could be seen, and later into a body that could be felt. A weak, pale analogy might be the change that takes place in water. When it is boiled it is changed into a different likeness and becomes steam. Later the steam becomes invisible and is vapour. And when that vapour encounters something cold—a windowpane, for example—it condenses and once more becomes water.

Some such thing as this took place, but the disciples could not believe, even though our Lord had told them that He would raise that body from the dead, would rebuild that temple of the body (John 2: 19–22). He had not told them plainly, in so many words, but in a figure of speech. There are many truths that Jesus does not tell us plainly in so many words. He leaves something to the imagination, or rather to the questing spirit of man, for if we do not strain and strive with every nerve to understand, if we do not ask and seek and knock upon the door of understanding, our souls do not grow.

Mary Magdalene turned about and saw Him standing there, in His body that was not yet quite material, if I may use that word. It was like Him and yet not like Him, as though she saw Him through a veil. As Jesus beheld her tears, He said to her, "Woman, why weepest thou? Whom seekest thou?"

Thinking Him to be the gardener or caretaker, she replied, "Sir, if thou hast borne Him hence, tell me where thou hast laid Him, and I will take Him away."

Jesus whispered to her, "Mary!"

Then she turned and cried, "Rabboni", which is to say, "Master."

As she said this she stretched out her hands toward Him. "Touch me not," He said, "for I am not yet ascended to my Father: but go to my brethren, and say unto them, I ascend unto my Father, and your Father; and to my God, and your God" (John 20: 15–17).

Why did He say, "Touch me not," except that His body was not as yet completely formed, had not as yet become solid, touchable? He had not yet received into Himself the full power of God. This was apparently taking place step by step, gradually, by a process which He knew. We think of

54

all these things as miraculous, and they are indeed miraculous, but they are not magic. There are behind all these phenomena laws that we do not yet understand but that in the long reaches of eternity we shall understand.

Furthermore, mysteriously, incredibly we are told that, "He that raised up Christ from the dead shall also quicken your mortal bodies by His Spirit that dwelleth in you" (Rom. 8: 11).

PRAYER

OH LORD, we give thanks for these gropings after a reality that is too great for us. And we pray that our spirits may be more and more uplifted and released into your spiritual kingdom so that we may be able to perceive whatever is good for us to perceive.

Enlighten us, Oh Lord, enlighten us, but most of all we pray that we will be able to see Jesus. Lord Jesus, you are the one whom we seek. And alas, in this dim world there are many who have taken you away, or have tried to take you away, calling you merely "the Christ-spirit within", or speaking of you as a man who lived some time ago, a great teacher, one of many masters, and not as the Son of God. They have taken away our Lord, and we know not where they have laid Him.

Oh Lord Jesus, appear to us as you did to Mary Magdalene. We cannot touch you at this time, not with our hands and perhaps not completely with our minds, but grant, Oh Lord, that with the inner eye of the spirit we may see you and know you as a living person here upon this earth, Amen.

9

A SPIRIT HATH NOT FLESH AND BONES . . .
Luke 24: 39

EVEN though our lives are drab and dim,
In heavenly places can we sit with Him,
   Even now—even now.

Therefore while our bodies stay on earth
That through the swing of aeons gave them birth,
Our souls can feel the heaven's joy and mirth,
   Even now—even now.

But this is not the end, for just as He
Appeared in flesh and bones for men to see,
Far in the shining of eternity
Resurrected bodies we shall be,
And so we shout and sing triumphantly,
   Even now—even now.

THE DISCIPLES WERE TERRIFIED and affrighted. They thought
that they were seeing a ghost when the risen Lord appeared to
them in Jerusalem, but He was not a ghost! He said, "Behold
my hands and my feet, that it is I myself: handle me, and
see" (Luke 24: 39).

Long before Jesus died and rose again an occasional prophet knew that there was a life after death. David was the first to suggest a concept of heaven; possibly he had glimpsed it. Were the green pastures and still waters limited to this earth? One does not know, but when his son by Bathsheba died, David said, "I shall go to him, but he shall not return to me" (2 Sam. 12: 23).

It was not necessary that Jesus should die the death of the cross and rise again merely to demonstrate life after death. His resurrection strengthens our belief, but the belief was already there. We are told that after the crucifixion the graves were opened and the spirits of many arose and went about the city, but Jesus most emphatically and explicitly stated that He was not a spirit.

What then are we to believe? Let us consider this matter head-on, straight-forward, without gloves or any kind of subterfuge. There are spirits, yes. A spirit is not the same as an angel. The spirit of a person who has lived in the flesh is, after his death, his essence or spiritual body living at a different rate of vibration in a different kind of world. Such spirits, if they find Jesus in that world, may rest in His peace and His joy, and perceive the beauties and glories of that life. If, however, they do not find Jesus, and if they have nothing in them wherewith to see and understand the spiritual kingdom, they may be lost and wandering. They may indeed be in torment, burnt up with the knowledge of what they have missed and now cannot find.

The risen Jesus who came to His disciples was not merely a spirit. The spirit of Jesus had departed immediately from His body when He said on the cross, "Father, into thy hands I commend my spirit," but His spirit returned again into the resurrected body. On the other hand, when the body of Lazarus was raised it was still a physical body, a human body, presumably subject to death at a later date, in contrast with the resurrected body of Jesus, which was a different

57

kind of body. It was a resurrection body, and the Church has always taught that we should all attain, some day, to the resurrection of the body. Jesus had said to the sisters of Lazarus, "Whosoever liveth and believeth in me shall never die" (John 11:26). Surely He meant more than merely the survival of spirit, for it is commonly accepted that the spirit even of a person who does not believe in Jesus does not die but remains, possibly to its great discomfiture.

Then what did Jesus mean? Now let us be very straightforward. I think the difference between a surviving spirit and a resurrected body is this: with a surviving spirit, the body is buried or cremated and goes back to dust; but with a resurrected body the body is transformed into its spiritual essence and disappears. It is not cremated; it is not buried. Now our Christian faith is based upon this stupendous concept: the body of Jesus did not remain in that tomb and turn to dust. St. Paul said, "If Christ be not raised, your faith is vain; ye are yet in your sins." And again he said, "If in this life only we have hope in Christ, we are of all men most miserable." And to cap the climax, he had the audacity to say, "Christ the firstfruits; afterward they that are Christ's at His coming" (1 Cor. 15: 17, 19, 23).

How and in what fashion His coming will be I do not know. He said, "Lo, I am with you always," and again He said that He would return at the latter days. In one sense His second coming has been accomplished at the day of Pentecost. In another sense it has not yet come, for He has not yet been seen visibly descending in the clouds as was foretold at His ascension (Acts 1: 11). Yet, without seeing it either with the eyes or with the mind, I believe that this shall be—that even though in the present day the body does die and turn to dust, yet nevertheless in the last day the surviving spirit will achieve or build for itself an identity.

There have been other instances of translation from one life to another life, shown us so that we may know even now that what Jesus will achieve some day for all men is not beyond belief. We are told that the prophet Elijah did not decay and turn to dust upon this earth but was carried up to heaven in an appearance as of a chariot of fire—an "unidentified flying object"? (2 Kings 2: 11). Elijah's body was caught up, as the risen body of Jesus was later caught up, and it disappeared in a spiritual light and a spiritual fire, and it was transformed without going through death.

St. Paul said that he longed to be transformed without going through death, to be clothed with a body that is from above, not to be unclothed from this mortal body (2 Cor. 5: 2). The Bible contains no account of the death of St. Paul. Tradition tells us that he was finally martyred, and yet I wonder: if he simply disappeared from the prison, would not the Roman government have said that he died? This is just wondering—but I like to wonder from time to time. I like to dream that his wish was granted.

Another man, Enoch, was translated. We are told that he walked with God, "and he was not, for God took him" (Gen. 5: 24). And possibly a third man; Moses' body arose quickly and went into the heavens, for there is a mystery about the death of Moses. We are told that God led him up into a mountain presumably alone, and there buried him, "but no man knoweth of his sepulchre unto this day" (Deut. 34: 5–6). How strange! Would not a great leader of his people normally have died among them and have been buried by them with deep mourning? We are told in another place that the archangel Michael contended with the devil over the body of Moses (Jude 9). Could it be that the body of Moses, like the body of Jesus, was raised again and does not remain upon this earth in the form of dust? Could that be the reason why, when our Lord was transfigured on the mountain, the two who appeared with Him were Moses and Elijah? I do not know.

But this I do know—that even as Jesus died and rose

again, so we dying shall rise again, the surviving spirit being clothed somehow in the far reaches of time with a resurrected body no longer subject to death.

We cannot know how this shall be. But if we keep our eyes upon Jesus it will be, for it is in Him and through Him that we shall enter into His glory.

Prayer

OH, LORD JESUS, help us to see! "We would see Jesus, for the shadows lengthen upon the little twilight of our life."

Oh, Lord Jesus, even though we cannot see you with these eyes of flesh, help us to see you with the eyes of the soul! Help us to believe not only that you died for us on the cross, but also that you arose again from the dead. And even more, help us to believe that since you arose again from the dead, some day, in some far kingdom, in some manner that we cannot understand, we also will be transformed and resurrected and become a new order of being—not just spirits, not merely ghosts, but resurrected sons of God, children of God, redeemed not only in the soul but also even in the body.

Help us, oh Lord God, to know and see your love incarnated in your Son, Jesus Christ, Our Lord, and through Him ever given unto us, Amen.

10

WHAT MANNER OF COMMUNICATIONS ... ?
Luke 24: 17

THEY KNEW HIM by the breaking of the bread,
And to this day we kneel upon our knees,
Reaching forth our hands to take the bread
That holds His body given for our sakes.
Oh mystery, that energy so great—
The radiation of the life of God—
Can enter into such a little thing,
And turn it into living sustenance
For body and for soul! The very Light
From which the worlds were made can shine anew—
Not to the eyes of flesh, but to the other eye
That sees beyond the flesh—into the cells
Of humble matter made of grains of wheat,
And plant in them the principle of life,
Ever expanding to the very doors
Of immortality! Oh wondrous love,
That He who blessed the bread at Emmaus
Holds within His hands the Bread of Life
That blesses all the world! Oh Lord of love
Help us who live so far away in time
To know You in the breaking of the bread!

LATER, ON THE DAY of Jesus' resurrection, there were two disciples walking to the little town of Emmaus. They were discussing Him, Jesus. As they talked Jesus Himself came and walked with them. "What manner of communications are these that ye have one to another, as ye walk, and are sad?" He asked them.

One of them replied, "Art thou only a stranger in Jerusalem, and hast not known the things which are come to pass there in these days?"

He said to them, "What things?"

They said, "Concerning Jesus of Nazareth, and how the chief priests and our rulers delivered Him to be condemned to death, and have crucified Him. Yea, and certain women also of our company made us astonished. They came saying that they had also seen a vision of angels, which said that He was alive. And certain of them which were with us went to the sepulchre, and found it even so as the women had said: but Him they saw not" (Luke 24: 13 ff.).

So they recounted to Him the matters that they had heard, and even as they tried to understand these things doubts were rising in their minds. The women had not said that they saw a *vision* of angels; they said that they saw angels. But these two disciples, rationalizing, dimmed it down to a vision of angels—a vision which might have been symbolic, or even imaginary.

The very One whom they were discussing was with them, but they were so intent upon their rationalizing and upon their intellectual speculations that they did not see Him. It is good that we use the minds that God has given us, and that we try to understand the great matters of God and of Jesus Christ, our Lord. Yet as we try to understand, using every power of the mind that we possess, we must not forget also to use the power of the spirit. This inner knowing comes forth from the deep levels of the being, instinctively. It is coaxed into life through the imagination, through the ability to wonder and even to conjecture. When we try to realize Jesus within the rational mind alone, we put Him into too small a compass. He can be standing beside us without our knowing it. But when we transcend the mind, and release the deeper and higher knowledge of the spirit, then we begin to perceive His presence.

As the two disciples walked with Him, Jesus expounded to them out of the Scriptures the words about Himself. For the Scriptures are full of Him, hidden beneath symbolism as in Genesis 3: 15, and told forth in the ringing words of inspired prophecy as in Isaiah 51. The history of man and of nations points again and again to the necessity of a redeemer —of God coming in a new way, veiled in flesh, to be not only with man but also in man through the power of His Holy Spirit.

If only Jesus Himself could walk beside us on the way of life, and expound these matters to our dull awareness, caked over as it is with materialism and so-called rationalism! And yet, we can call upon His Spirit even thus to walk beside us on the way and to open to us the inner meaning of the Scriptures, so that we can see not only the prophecies of His redemptive act on Calvary but also the need and value of this redemptive power for the healing of our own deep minds.

Even as Jesus walked beside the disciples, and Himself explained to them many things in the Bible, they still did not recognize Him. And so it can be today. I have known many so-called Christ-centred and consecrated people, who knew the Bible from start to finish and who could expound dogma, doctrine and theology world without end, and who yet did not know Him. And this fact of which they were grievously unaware was glaringly apparent to their husbands or wives and even their children, and to those who worked with them, because the love of Jesus was not in their hearts.

63

Evening drew near and the two disciples asked Jesus to come in and have supper with them, saying, "Abide with us, for it is toward evening and the day is far spent." As He sat at meat with them, He took bread and blessed it and broke it and gave it to them. Their eyes were opened and they knew Him, and He vanished out of their sight.

Their eyes were opened. Was it merely because when He lifted His hands to break the bread they could see the wounds in His hands? I do not think so. If it had been thus, the Bible would have said that they saw the wounds in His hands. But it did not. It said, "And their eyes were opened." That is, their understanding was enlightened. If there had been wounds visible in His hands, surely they would have noticed them as they walked and talked upon the way. His body was under His control, and He was perfecting it moment by moment and hour by hour. As He perfected it, apparently it was possible for the wounds to become visible when He so desired, and at other times to be invisible.

The eyes of the disciples' understanding were opened when, having done what they could with the rational mind, they ceased to talk, and prayed. Even the simple prayer of asking a blessing on their meal merged their spirits so that they perceived a reality which all their talk had not shown them.

So it is. When we cease to talk, and even to study the Bible, and turn to the Lord of life Himself, and listen quietly while He blesses us, then we know Him. Again and again the answer that we have not found in discussion and study comes to us in prayer, entering from His Spirit into the unconscious mind, and then, when we are quiet enough and are listening, coming up into the conscious.

There is an old story concerning the eminent divines who met to put together the Westminster Shorter Catechism, a tremendous statement concerning God and man. (Born of Presbyterian parents on the mission field, I had to memorize this catechism in early childhood. Even my conscious mind still remembers many of those great, simple statements about God and His laws, and how many of them remain as a reservoir of strength and wisdom in the unconscious I do not know.) One question stopped them: "What is God?" They discussed it in long committee meetings, and studied the Bible, looking for inspiration, but they did not find it. Finally one of them said, "Brethren, let us pray." So they knelt, and he began: "Oh God, thou who art a Spirit infinite, eternal and unchangeable in thy being, wisdom, power, holiness, justice, goodness and truth——" And the prayer was answered before it was completed. As soon as they stopped talking, and opened their minds to God, He gave them the words of majesty and simplicity, which to this day are in the catechism and in the hearts of many believers.

God is near to bishops and archbishops as they sit in solemn conclave at a committee meeting. If only they will cease their endless discussions and kneel and pray and listen to Him, no doubt He will give them answers such as they have never found in all their talking. He is near to little children struggling to remember some historic date, for instance, and it can be that if they think of God and of the life of Jesus, His Son, and say within themselves, "Oh Lord, help me to remember!" the answer will float easily into their conscious minds.

God is near to this created earth that groans and travails, waiting for His sons to reveal Him to it, so that it may be set free from the bondage of corruption into the glorious liberty of the sons of God (Rom. 8: 21). Moreover, we are commanded to tell of His love to every creature (Mark 16: 15).

A year ago I lost a beloved brother, following a crippling automobile accident. While struggling to regain the use of his limbs he had to cease engineering and took to painting, which he did with great zest. He had never studied painting, but he opened his mind to the source of creativity, and painted what the Lord showed him to paint. His constant companion was a beautiful and highly bred cat who would sit on his shoulder and watch him work. After he had died the cat would wait long hours at the window for his car to come up the road, and if there were footsteps at the front door the poor animal would dart there all aquiver, hoping it would be the man she loved. This distressed my sister-in-law and she mentioned it to the people from whom she had bought the cat.

"Well, have you told her that he died?" they asked.

"No, I never thought of that."

"You must tell her," said the former owners of the cat, "and then she will be satisfied."

My sister-in-law took the cat in her lap and said to her very slowly, "The One who made you, made Him, and he has gone to be with Him." And the cat apparently understood, for she no longer waited for the return of her master, and was contented.

This may sound utterly foolish, and yet the most advanced scientists are beginning to tell us of the deep, veiled understanding of living things, and not only animals but also plants that live on love, and shrivel and die on hate.

The disciples at Emmaus did not themselves bless the bread. Jesus lifted up His hands and blessed the bread, and perhaps also the field of wheat from which the bread was made. As He blessed the bread they felt again the impact of His love, and then they remembered how their hearts had burned within them, quickened by divine love and life, as He walked beside them on the way. And they knew Him.

As we turn to Him in prayer and ask Him to bless the bread we eat and the land from which it comes, His love indeed goes forth, and who knows how far that love can shine? As more and more of us live in His love and in His light, and do His works of blessing and healing, of resurrection and prayer, we also will know Him more and more. With the inner eye of the soul we will see Him. And then shall the earth bring forth her increase, and all the ends of the earth shall bless Him.

PRAYER

OH LORD, we pray that the eyes of our understanding may be opened. We pray that we may know Jesus not only with the mind but also with the inner light of the spirit. We pray also that we may understand from the Scriptures the mysterious truths about Jesus, and the reasons why He had to come into the world.

May we search and find and be illumined! May the eyes of our understanding be opened more and more! And may we more and more see Jesus as He walks with us! Amen.

11

LOVEST THOU ME?
John 21: 15

How CAN I, LORD? I cannot see your face,
Nor touch the hand that once was pierced for me.
My heart is like a bird within a cage,
That cannot lift its wings and fly beyond
The realm of sight and sound. If I could see
Your gentle face—if I could hear your voice—
Then would my heart leap out beyond its cage,
And fly to love you, Lord. "Feed my lambs."
"But Lord you know I love you——" "Feed my sheep."
"Only I cannot feel it——" "Feed my sheep."
"Yes. I hear you, Lord. Only those
Who feed your creatures with the bread of life,
So that they live anew—only those
Who love in deed, my Lord, love you in truth."

"LOVEST THOU ME?" This was the last question that our Lord asked one of His disciples while He was on earth. He asked it of Peter, and the manner of His asking was this. The disciples went fishing, and that night they caught nothing. "But when the morning was now come, Jesus stood on the shore: but the disciples knew not that it was Jesus. Then

Jesus saith unto them, Children, have ye any meat? They answered him, No. And he said unto them, Cast the net on the right side of the ship, and ye shall find. They cast therefore, and now they were not able to draw it for the multitude of fishes . . . As soon then as they were come to land, they saw a fire of coals there, and fish laid thereon, and bread. Jesus saith unto them, Bring of the fish which ye have now caught. Simon Peter went up, and drew the net to land full of great fishes, an hundred and fifty and three: and for all there were so many, yet was not the net broken" (John 21: 4–6, 9–11).

Thus the story begins—a fantastic story. The fish obeyed His word and went where He told them to go. The net was supernaturally strengthened so that it did not break. There appeared on the seashore a breakfast cooked on coals of fire; whether He brought the coals of fire in a brazier or whether He, being the Creator, simply summoned them into life, we do not know.

Why did He manifest His power in things of nature? He made no explanation. He simply showed them that all power in heaven and earth was indeed given to Him, and that things on the earth that have minds and think, and things that, as far as we know, do not have rational minds are subject to His will and obedient to His voice.

We might wonder in a childish way about the fish that gave up their lives that the disciples might eat. In this present earth the sacrifice of a lower order of life for a higher order goes all the way through nature—plants to animals, animals to man—and will do so until man, made in the image and likeness of God, is sufficiently filled with the spirit of God to re-charge, revitalize, transform and resurrect the body which is from above. When and how the manner of this will be we do not yet know.

Did the fish hear the voice of Jesus and obey Him? Certainly they did! As we have already seen, there is

69

rudimentary intelligence in every cell of the body. Not in their conscious minds but in an unconscious or instinctive feeling the fish did hear the word of the Lord and they did obey Him.

Was the net strengthened that it did not break? Certainly it was! I have known of miraculous escapes, wonderful savings of life, that took place in this same way, by the superimposition of a spiritual power on a material object. I have known, for instance, of an aeroplane that from the human point of view would inevitably crash, with two engines stopped and very little petrol, being held up mysteriously in the sky and taken to its appointed destination.

Of course no one can prove such things, yet I have heard story after story from people who believe and know that a spiritual power entered into a material substance for the saving of life, and as an act of love.

Even more amazing than His control of the fish and the net was Jesus' production of a real fire of coals on which the fish were cooked. How did He get those burning coals? Can we imagine Him going to the market-place and buying coal and tinder? Hardly. Apparently He, the Lord of life, and of heaven and earth, had the power to precipitate from the divine image existing in the air, from the archetype of coal, the factual presence of coal, and to cause it to burn.

If this power belongs to Jesus, and if Jesus gave this power to us (John 14: 12), why can we not also do such miracles as this in His name? I think the answer is obvious. We are not sufficiently wise, not sufficiently unselfish. We cannot be entrusted with such power. We do perform miracles of transformation and of creation, indeed, but for the most part we do them with such means as bulldozers and nuclear reactors.

Then when shall we be ready for such power as Jesus used on that seashore? Let us continue with the story, and perhaps we shall see. Jesus said to Peter, "Lovest thou me?"

using the highest and strongest word for love, *agape*. Peter answered, "Yea, Lord, thou knowest that I love thee," using a smaller word for love, *philia*. Again Jesus said, "Lovest thou me?" using the greater word, and again Peter answered using the smaller word. The third time Jesus asked him, this time using the smaller word, as if to say, "I know that you cannot yet encompass the greater love, but do you at least love me in this little way?" And Peter said, "Thou knowest that I love thee."

Each time Peter said, "Thou knowest that I love thee," the Lord said to him, "Feed my lambs. Feed my sheep. Feed my sheep." This is the way that we show our love for Jesus, by feeding with spiritual food His little lambs and His sheep.

It is only when we do this out of love for Jesus, as well as out of concern for the individual, that His power is free to flow. People have sometimes said to me, "Oh, do pray for Mrs. So-and-So. You know she is very wealthy and influential, and if she were only healed, what a wonderful thing it would be for the church!" That never works. Although we may not realize it, the motive is not the right motive. There is a certain desire to show off, to prove, to force truth upon someone.

Only one motive is a sound motive, and that is the love of Jesus. From that grows another motive, smaller and part of the first, and that is of course love for the individual, love for the helpless little lamb, or for the obstinate old sheep. As we feed His sheep, His love is poured out upon us more and more until at last we are lifted into the greater love, *agape*, divine love, the kind of love that forever and always "seeketh not its own". This love is the spiritual reactor from which power comes.

And it may be that the salvation of our little earth depends upon the evolving of this divine love that feeds His sheep and feeds His lambs. There are prophecies of the earth being destroyed by fire. There are also prophecies of its becoming the Kingdom of our God and of His Christ.

Which will it be? It must be one or the other: love or perish.

✠

PRAYER

OH LORD, we pray that we may be so filled with Thy love that we will recognize the needs of Thy little lambs and Thy sheep when we see them. Let us hear Thy voice saying, "This one is hungry for me. This one is thirsty for the water of life. Feed my lambs. Feed my sheep."

We give thanks, oh Lord, that our love of Thee is more than an emotion. Some of us can feel the warmth and passion of Thy love in our hearts, and some of us cannot feel it. We cannot control our feelings, but we can control our actions. We give thanks, oh Lord, that to us is given the joy and the glory of showing our love for Thee by feeding Thy sheep. Yet we long also for the deep comfort and the unreasoning ecstasy of the feeling of Thy love within our hearts. We pray thee, oh Lord, that as we feed Thy flock our hearts may be rejoiced and our spirits up-lifted by Thy most precious gift of love, Amen.

12

SPIRIT AND FIRE
Acts 1: 5

WHAT HAS become of the fire? It is lost; it is gone!
Never again is the door of a prison unlocked
By an angel who bears in his hand an invisible flame—
Will never again a cripple arise to his feet,
And enter the temple of God with a run and a leap?
Where is the shadow of Peter that fell on the crowd,
Healing the people who lay upon cots on the street?
Or Philip transported afar by the Spirit of God,
Returning he did not know how in a flash to his home?
Gone—it is gone! And longing we clamour aloud,
"Power! We must have power! Machinery! Science!"
Everything else but the fire of the Spirit of God.
Fire of creation—fire of eternity—come!
With spirit, with heart, and with longing we call for the fire
To burn in the hearts of mankind and to bring into life
The makers of peace upon earth—the children of God!

"YE SHALL BE BAPTIZED with the Holy Ghost not many days
hence" (Acts 1: 5). These were the key words of our Lord's
last talk with His disciples while in a visible body on the
earth. Then that body was transformed, and as it was

73

transformed it rose. It changed its nature, gradually being lifted into the air, until a cloud received it out of their sight. This might have been a natural cloud of moisture, such as we see in the sky, or it might have been a cloud of light, the shining forth of the effulgence of His own brightness as His body was changed into the glorified body of the Son of God.

As He was received out of their sight, two men in white apparel stood by the disciples and said to them, "Ye men of Galilee, why stand ye gazing up into heaven? This same Jesus, which is taken up from you into heaven, shall so come in like manner as ye have seen Him go into heaven" (Acts 1: 11).

These who spoke with such authority and power were not men of earth. They were angels or else resurrected ones, ones who had already attained the resurrection body. They showed themselves, however, not with countenances like lightning, not with vast shining wings, but in a simple way, merely as men clothed in white garments. And they said comfortingly that He would return again.

The physical body of Jesus had been transmuted into light and hidden in a cloud of light, and they would see it no more. But His spiritual body was soon to return to them in that upper room where they had been awaiting Him for ten days. It was not to the multitude that He returned, not to the scribes and Pharisees. Those who saw His glory were not a cross-section of the community, nor were they the religious leaders of the day. They were His friends, trained in His service, those who had obeyed and followed Him through life to death, and through death to life again.

As they waited, His Holy Spirit came upon them with a sound like a rushing mighty wind, and with a burning energy actually visible as it entered them through the doorway of the head (the centre of understanding), like cloven tongues of fire.

They caught on fire! Hidden and submerged emotions and

powers within them were suddenly released, and they were filled with such ecstasy that people thought they were drunk! The other half of the personality—the spiritual body —could not live and breathe and act and speak, even in the midst of this earthly life, in the power and glory of the heavenly life from which it came, and where it would return, and where it lived!

It was a breakthrough into a new level of consciousness, into a new state of existence. A caterpillar, slow and often ugly, crawls on the ground, goes into a pupa state, and after a time bursts through its cocoon as a new creature with wings. It no longer crawls on the ground or a leaf, but flies in the air. It no longer sees only the bit of earth or grass beneath its head, but glimpses sun and sky and the beauty of trees and flowers as far away as it can see. Yet everything in the butterfly was already there, potentially, in the caterpillar.

Cloven tongues of light, of flame, descended upon every person in the upper room at Pentecost. They had seen this light in Jesus. They had beheld His glory, the glory as of the only begotten of the Father. Three of them had seen Him totally illumined by this light on the mount of transfiguration. All had seen Him ascend into a cloud of that same light ever-increasing when He removed the veil from His being; and His physical body, ascending, was completely caught up, transmuted and transformed into the resurrection body lit by the Spirit.

Now they saw this glory, His glory, descending upon every one of them! Each must have felt the burning of that holy fire, even as I have felt it more than once, like a coal of fire burning in the head, as the disciples at Emmaus felt it in their hearts when He walked beside them. Now they *saw* that light! They themselves beheld the glory of Jesus, and furthermore they saw it enter into every one of them!

Jesus had said that He would return to them. He had

also said that the Father in His name (that is, in His personality, for in Scriptures the name means the personality, the being) would send the comforter, the Holy Spirit. Was this the manner of His returning—that His Holy Spirit should enter into and inhabit their bodies?

Something came into them, spirit, mind and body. Power hitherto impossible to them now surged into life. They found themselves speaking to the multitude that quickly gathered round them, drawn by their excitement and their overwhelming joy, as the upper room could no longer contain their glory and they burst forth into the open air. As they spoke to those of all nations who ran together, as people will to behold a happening, they spoke in different languages, so that all the people understood. They must have wondered with heart-shaking amazement how this could be, but even as they wondered they spoke tongues that their conscious minds did not know but that another mind stirring within them did know. Surely! For Christ had indeed come again, in the first step of His coming, and they now had the mind of Christ! He, being from the beginning the Son of God and the son of man, knew every tongue spoken upon earth and in heaven, even so could they in Him speak as the Spirit guided them in tongues utterly unknown to their conscious minds.

Some of you may be thinking that this is impossible. Not at all. I have myself heard an ordinary young woman with no conscious knowledge of the language speaking perfect Hebrew, as a seminary professor listening to her testified. I have heard another woman (she did not know Arabic) speaking Arabic, which a former missionary heard and understood. These incidents, however, are rare, for usually the tongue in which one speaks by the inspiration of the Spirit is unknown both to the speaker and to anyone listening. The main purpose in this "holy talking", as a friend of mine called it, is not to convince the multitude but to edify the speaker. And so it does, for since he is speaking by the inspiration of the Spirit he is closer to God, and the effect of this closeness is felt in his peace and joy, and in his increase in wisdom and guidance.

We read in the New Testament of no other gathering together of the multitude to see and hear these phenomena, for the disciples soon learned that the real purpose of God speaking through His Holy Spirit was to testify not to the gifts of the Christians but to the reality of Jesus.

Therefore far more sensational than this gift of speaking in unknown tongues was the inspiration of the Holy Spirit on Peter that caused him to testify of Jesus with such stunning force that three thousand people were converted in one day.

Could something like this possibly be true of us? It can. The gifts of the Spirit discussed extensively in my book* on that subject exist, potentially, in every one of us. Moreover, they have already been given to each Christian in his baptism, but they are burning low. Or perhaps they are not burning at all, like a fire already laid to which no match has been applied. We are capable of far more wisdom and knowledge, discernment and faith than we ordinarily use. Our bits of carefully learned faith in healing and miracles can be tremendously increased by the Holy Spirit. Even the more mysterious gifts—tongues, interpretation, prophecy— are not magic but are the explosion within us of latent powers. The Spirit can so move us that we can speak a language known only to the subconscious mind. Even more profitably, the Spirit can speak through us in our native tongue with power and eloquence hitherto unknown to us.

The possibility of making this breakthrough into a new life lies in every one of us. This indeed is the purpose of the sacrament of confirmation: that the Holy Spirit given to a child in

*Healing Gifts of the Spirit, published by Arthur James of Evesham, Worcs.

baptism shall at this time explode into a new life within him, and thus the grace of God shall increase in him more and more. When this happens, confirmation is a never-to-be-forgotten experience for young people. But more often it fails to go off, like a firecracker without a fuse. Why? Because people, priests and bishops lack the fuse of expectancy. They do not believe that such a release of personality can really take place. Or perhaps, having seen certain instances when the gift of tongues was received without the gift of wisdom, they not without reason fear such an experience.

If, however, we have missed it in the formal way of confirmation, we can still receive the experience when two or three (or more) are gathered together in prayer and earnest seeking for this baptism of the Holy Spirit and fire. Indeed, if only we know that what we have of Christ is not enough— that there is more light and joy and power available to us— it is possible to receive this spiritual experience alone. But ordinarily, as in the New Testament (for instance, Acts 2: 1–4, 8: 14–17, 10: 44), the Spirit explodes in a group of those who seek Him. There are many such groups, and one can only pray that the Lord will guide one's questing feet in the right direction, for although the most sensational of the gifts of the Spirit (1 Cor. 12) is tongues, yet without wisdom and knowledge that gift can be disturbing to some people.

The glory that can be revealed to us (Romans 8) is so tremendous that to some it is frightening, and to others it is repellent and therefore does not win them to Christ but pushes them away. Do not, therefore, feel that you must needs testify in words if you have had this experience. It is often better to keep this holy secret within yourself until husband or wife or friend or pastor says, "What has happened to you? You're so different, so free, so happy. What is it?" Then you can know that you have testified in the way that is most sound, most convincing—by your life, by your self, by your being. For you are a new creature in Christ Jesus, and those who know you see it and rejoice.

PRAYER

LORD JESUS, we have followed you through the seven words that you spoke upon the cross, and we have followed you all the way from Calvary to Pentecost. We have meditated upon the words that you spoke to your disciples after your resurrection. How wonderful that you showed yourself only to those who believed in you, only to those who loved you! You did not burst upon Pontius Pilate and say, "Lo, here I am!" So we should show forth your power only for love of you, and for love of your children. Then you yourself, oh Lord, will show yourself in ways that we do not know.

We pray, therefore, Lord Jesus, that your Holy Spirit may enter into us more and more. Perhaps this heavenly light and power will burst upon us some time when we worship with a group. Perhaps someone who is filled with the Spirit will lay hands upon us, and a door will open in our minds, and we will feel the warm inflow of your love. Or perhaps only in our own daily seeking, our own quiet waiting upon you, the power will increase and increase until some day there will be a breakthrough into a new area of being.

We do not know how the Holy Spirit will come upon us, but we do know, Lord Jesus, that for this purpose, that we might be baptized with the Holy Ghost, you gave your life upon the cross.

Forgive us, oh Lord, that we have supinely said, "Oh, we have no power. We have no responsibility. God can do everything." For we do have the responsibility of being your agents and obeying your words. And we do have the power to take the sword of the spirit which is the word of God, and so to speak and move upon this earth that miracles shall happen, those glorious miracles that are not the breaking of laws but the bringing forth of spiritual laws that we have not as yet known.

And we give thanks, oh Lord, that your power is in every created thing—every rock and every stone, every tree and every bush, every flying bird and every little creeping creature, and every son of man who is born upon this earth. And all are bound up in your light, and all are bound up in your love, and the time will come when you will deliver back the kingdom to the Father, Amen.

13

YE SHALL RECEIVE POWER
Acts 1: 8

HE SAID that He would come again. He came,
  Departing in a shining cloud of light,
And coming back in cloven tongues of flame.
  And He is here, though hidden from our sight.

Quicken, Lord, our eyes that we may see
  Lingering glory as Thy footsteps pass,
Auras of light surrounding every tree,
  And shining on the flowers and on the grass.

And may our hearts be lit with holy joy,
  Our cloven natures healed with tongues of fire,
That by Thy power we may bring to birth,
A kingdom that no power can destroy—
  Redeemed and cleansed and lifted from the mire;
  Thy kingdom here upon this little earth.

✠

WE HAVE INDEED RECEIVED the power of God. This power is
God's very breath, the breath of life that He breathed into
man in the beginning, thus making him a living soul (Gen.
2: 7). It is our birthright, and the birthright of all men,

though rejected by Adam and rejected long since by the race of mankind because they could not stand the full glory of it, because they were not able to lift up their eyes unto the hills of eternity, but preferred to crawl upon the ground, seeing only the earth.

Those who have seen this glory with the inner eye have built it into soaring cathedrals that to this day uplift the heart of the wondering beholder. They have spread it on canvas in paintings full of light, speaking in silent words beneath and beyond the form of the painting. They have expressed it in that sound of music that rings with immortality. Most wonderful of all, they have woven it into the warp and woof of the soul, attaining to greatness and power not so much by the solving of inner problems as by transcending them.

It is God's will that this power of His Spirit shall bring to the earth a kingdom of heaven, and for this we are commanded to pray. It is His will that this glory shine to the very ends of the earth, and that every creature that lives walk in the light of it (Rev. 5: 13).

The prophet Isaiah wrote: "Arise, shine; for thy light is come, and the glory of the Lord is risen upon thee" (Is. 60: 1). In His light is power, as in the radiation of electricity there is power either to create visible light or to cause things to move. This power belongs to God and comes from God, but by His will, by the intervention of Jesus Christ, and by the operation of the Holy Spirit, it is given to us that we may use it in His service. We are His stewards. We are the keepers of His vineyards, the managers of His estates, the transactors of His business upon earth, as Jesus has often told us in parables. For us to say, "Oh, I have no power. God can do everything," is as unreasonable as it would be for a bank clerk to sit with folded hands and say, "I have no power. All things belong to the manager." If the clerks did this, all banks would soon lose their business and close their doors.

And if all Christians do this, the time will come when churches will close their doors.

The branches of a grapevine cannot bring forth fruit unless they are connected with the vine, as Jesus taught us (John 15). Nor can the vine bear fruit without the branches. God needs those of us who are filled with His Spirit to be the conveyors of His power upon earth. If we love Him, therefore, we will not set Him aside and trust only in education, science and politics to bring the kingdom of heaven on earth. Nor will we stand idly by, saying, "I am weak and small and can do nothing." Rather we will take and use this power that He was at such infinite pains to give us. We will use it out of love for Him. We will feed His lambs and feed His sheep, out of love for Him. All over the world people are dying for lack of this heavenly hope, dying in body and in spirit. Yet there is little use in our saying to them, "God can save your soul and your spirit," unless there is such power going from us that by our act of prayer and faith this power moves in them toward healing and life.

As soon as the Holy Spirit came upon those who awaited Him at Pentecost they became conveyors of His power on earth. They became the branches who brought forth the fruit of the Spirit. They not only had the mind of Christ, but they also had the healing hands of Christ. Probably they did not know this in the beginning—not until the occasion for healing arose.

Peter and John saw a man lame from birth sitting at the gate of the temple begging alms. Perhaps Peter thought in an agony of compassion, "If only Jesus were here to stretch forth His hands and heal this man!" And perhaps Jesus said within his mind, "Then stretch them forth, and heal him!" So Peter said to the man, "In the name of Jesus Christ of Nazareth, arise and walk."

Even while Christ was on earth the disciples had done miracles, but some things were too difficult for them and required the healing touch of Jesus Himself. Surely no healing would require more faith and more spiritual power than the healing by word alone of a man born lame! Yet at Peter's command the man arose and entered with them into the temple, walking and leaping and praising God. Can you not see the picture?

When people asked Peter how this came to pass, he replied that the name of Jesus had healed the man (Acts 3: 16). Peter did not know the difference. As he had the mind of Christ so that he could speak languages that Christ knew and his conscious mind did not know, so also through faith in the name of Christ he had His healing hands.

God often speaks to us in dreams. Long ago, I had a dream that is as real to me now as it was then. I was walking on a little path around the house where I had first received the Holy Spirit. It was night, but I saw on the path a huddled thing, lying not directly along the path but across it. And I said in the dream, "Oh, it's dead!" Then I felt a lightning-flash of power entering into me between the shoulders and tingling down my spine. And I said, "In the name of Jesus Christ of Nazareth, arise and walk!" The thing arose, and it was a man. The flesh grew upon it, colour flamed in its face, light came into its eyes, and it became tall and beautiful. It stood right in the middle of the path, and it walked.

If ever I were to feel in real life that stroke of power down the spine, I would sense it as the authority to say what Peter said to the lame man. Yet this dream, as interpreted to me, means more than that. The man was the Church of Christ, not actually dead but moribund for lack of power. Through re-education in the power of Christ the Church was to arise, come to life, stand in the middle of the path of life, and walk. That day has not yet come, but it is coming.

What is this power that can cause a lame man to arise and walk, and a lame Church to stand right in the middle of the pathway of life and walk in light and joy? It is Jesus in us and working through us, for if He is completely in us, filling the total being with His being, then He must do His works through us. This is His nature, and if His life is flowing freely through us, then the fruits of that life will be seen in the world around us. If the life of a vine is flowing freely through a branch, then that branch will bring forth fruit. When a branch brings forth no fruit, then, as Jesus said, it is cut off and it withers and dies.

If the disciples had merely continued to meet and speak in tongues, and to tell others about that ecstatic experience and draw them into it, Christianity might have died out in a few years. It was the wonderful works that followed Pentecost—as when Peter went down the street, and even his shadow passing by healed the sick—that showed forth and spread the power of God.

Let me now meditate upon an ancient apple tree beside the old farmhouse in New Hampshire which for many years was the home of my soul. White lilies and ferns nestled at the foot of this old tree, and robins built their nests in its branches. Its snowy blossoms shone like a gentle light among the pale green trees of early spring, and then scattered among the dewdrops on the ground beneath it, over trilliums and ferns, lilies of the valley and wild violets, all growing casually among rough grass. Later the apples also fell to the ground. They were far too many for me to use, and some of them belonged to the insects that shared the land with me. There they lay and decayed, their rich warm smell mingling with the fragrance of pine trees and mown grass. Their life entered into the ground from which they came, and enriched it so that the old tree grew and brought forth more apples; it needed no fertilizer save the spreading of its own richness upon the ground.

So do miracles of healing and faith fall upon the ground of life, enriching and nourishing it with God's love, so that the fruit of His love and compassion may more and more spread over the earth. A church that is so fed with His creativity needs less and less of the artificial fertilizer of programmes, drives, canvasses and committees, for the fruits of the love of Jesus abiding in its people fall upon the very ground of life, sweetening and enriching it so that yet more fruit abounds.

The fire of the Spirit has burned low in the Church; the fruits of the Spirit, brought forth by the gifts of the Spirit, have dwindled and faded away. Yet they have never altogether ceased, and nowadays when men are very weary of the dullness of rationality they are ripening more and more. To-day many simple people stretch forth the hand to heal. For instance, a little girl who had learned of healing in a summer school stole into the bedroom where her baby brother lay in the fever of a violent disease, and stretched forth her hands into the crib and laid them upon him, trusting Jesus to make him well. And when the ambulance came for the infant he was perfectly whole again.

A child of six, lame since birth, sat in her wheelchair in a religious school where the teacher sang with the juniors the little poems in my book *Let's Believe*.* As they sang, the child said to her teacher, "I think I can get out of this chair and walk." The teacher, who believed in Jesus, calmly replied, "Well, why don't you try it, dear?" The little girl did walk a few steps then, and now she no longer needs the wheelchair.

Those who did these little miracles had not known the experience of Pentecost with its rushing wind and tongues of flame. They had only the measure of the Holy Spirit passed on to them in a gentle and perhaps unconscious way through their church. What would happen if these, and many like them, should go on to receive the augmenting of this simple power of child-like faith by a further explosion of the life of Jesus within them—the baptism of His Spirit? And what would happen if all of those filled, as they like to say, with

*Let's Believe, published by Arthur James of Evesham, Worcs.

His Spirit would also learn the simple, child-like faith to obey His commandments and to do His works?

Surely we would have a kingdom of heaven on earth!

PRAYER

ALL POWER in heaven and earth is given to you, oh Lord Jesus Christ—the power to recreate, even as in the beginning you sent forth the word of God and out of darkness there was created light—the power to heal even as you healed on earth when the lame walked, the blind saw and the deaf heard, so that here and there splinters of light from the kingdom of heaven shone on the earth.

You have chosen us on whom the Holy Spirit has descended to be channels of this light—light-bearers, high and lifted up like a city that cannot be hid for the light that is in it. May this healing light now be increased in us who pray. We reach out into the air around us and draw to us by faith the energy of this light-power. Now we picture this light shining out of us into the world, piercing the darkness here and there, as far as it will go. Into this light we lift up the one for whom we pray, and by faith we picture your light, Lord Jesus, entering into him and beginning a healing which shall continue until he is restored to that wholeness of soul, mind and body that we believe is your will for him.

And now, oh Lord, we also hold up your Church, the blessed company of all believers, through which the Holy Spirit was released to shine upon all the earth. May your light enter anew into the Church, awakening therein faith, hope, joy and love. We lift up before you the seminaries where young ministers are trained to do your work. Drive out of them, oh Lord, the spirit of materialism and false teaching, even as you drove the money changers out of the temple of

Jerusalem. Let these modern money changers be shaken and awakened by a rush of your active power, Lord Jesus. Appear before them through their closed doors, even as you appeared to the disciples in their closed upper room. So let them once more know that you are Lord and King!

Let your ministers go forth in joy and power to save and to heal, proclaiming to all that the kingdom of heaven has indeed come nigh unto them! Amen.

14

GO YE INTO ALL THE WORLD
Mark 16: 15

IT CANNOT WAIT forever, tortured earth,
The blood of Abel crying from the ground
Unavenged—still unavenged—alas!
What shall stop its crying? Death again?
Other Abels killed for Abel's blood,
Until the very earth is filled with blood,
Its rivers running red? It cannot wait!
It is *alive*, the earth on which we stand
And breed corruption till its horrid stench
Fills all the sea and sky! The creature moves!
Groaning and travailing the while it waits
To see the sons of the creator God
Bearing gifts of love within their hands,
For only love can heal it—only love.
It cannot wait forever! It will rise
And shake away the vermin, hateful man,
With all his slow corruption, from its breast,
Unless we go, as He commanded us,
And tell to all the world that God is love.
To little birds that fly I tell it then:
God is love. To squirrels on my lawn;
And rabbits nibbling in my flower beds;
To wild coyotes, lonely on the hills;

And deer who shine at night from out the dark,
As headlights touch their horns; to rattlesnakes
Deep within my canyon; and to all
The tiny things that chirp within the grass—
"God is love, and I, in Jesus' name,
Declare His love to you whom He has made."
And to the mountains as they thunder high
In wild cascades of rocks from plain to sky,
To them I cry, "Be comforted—be still—
Forgive the sins of man, as we forgive
Man and the ghastly world that they have made,
By pouring out the love of Jesus Christ
Given to heal the whole created world."
And to the faults beneath the earth I say,
"Gently, quiver gently down below,
And let the dim foundations of the deep,
The ocean's floor, remember little man,
Whom she has nourished on her flowing breast,
And sing to him a lullaby of peace,
Moving softly lest her offspring die
Beneath a lethal rush of tidal wave.
Go into all the world—to all the world—
And tell to every creature, God is love!"

HE SAID: "Go ye into all the world, and preach the gospel to
every creature" (Mark 16: 15). But they did not go anywhere,
and shortly afterwards He disappeared before their very eyes
in a cloud of light; and they saw Him no more. There they
were alone, deserted, helpless, with an impossible task laid
upon their shoulders—the task of making known to every
creature the infinite love of God.

A few days later they had a committee meeting and
elected Matthias to take the place of Judas and fill the ranks

of the disciples. That, however, is the last we hear of Matthias, for God had already chosen Paul to be the last of the apostles, and without anyone casting lots or deciding, so Paul became. The gospel could not be preached to every creature, nor could the kingdom of heaven come merely by having a committee meeting but only by the breaking forth of the Holy Spirit.

And the Holy Spirit came at Pentecost, ushered in by wind and fire, filling the disciples with the power of God. They went forth to all the regions round about the Mediterranean Sea and to India, to the British Isles, and to China, to tell to every creature that God is love, shown to us through Jesus Christ. The earth was enriched and sweetened by the pure love of God shining in the face of Jesus Christ, as the ground around my apple tree was enriched and sweetened by fallen fruit, that it might bring forth more fruit. But as from time to time wild creatures came and ate my apples, attracted by their fragrance, so the fragrance of the goodness of Jesus Christ attracted the enemy who came to destroy and to despoil that which the love of Jesus had made good.

Jesus knew that this would be, and that the kingdom of heaven on earth would not be won without danger and sorrow, persecution and death. In His own person He conquered Satan, and therefore as He abides in us we also can win by His strength the battle against evil. But that does not mean that there is no battle, no struggle, no gruelling necessity for choice. Jesus told us that there would be much tribulation before His kingdom would be perfectly established on earth. There would be a great battle of good against evil. There would be plagues and famines. There would be terror by night and by day, and men would hide in holes in the ground lest destruction rain upon them from the skies above. Nevertheless, He said, when we see these signs we are to lift up our heads, for our redemption is drawing nigh.

We are to lift up our heads in hope. We are to lift up

our heads in joy and in triumph, for the new Jerusalem is drawing near to the earth, and in that holy city the Lord Himself will be such a light to all people that even the sun and the moon will not be needed. We are to pray and work toward that day of the Lord. So He ordered us to pray, and His command remains: "Thy kingdom come, thy will be done, on earth as it is in heaven." As we pray, we must believe that this shall be, or our prayers have no power. Those who believe that the earth will be destroyed and all people with it save only themselves, the elect, are not keeping His command to pray for the kingdom, the holy city, to be established on earth.

He said that there would be great tribulations, certainly. If He had not warned us that this must be, until the power of evil is totally destroyed, then we would have lost faith long ago. He told us of all these things—earthquake, fire and flood—but He also ordered us to pray for His kingdom to come.

As we remain faithful and pray, we often find to our amazement that His love through our faith has power even on the forces of evil, for they cannot touch us, as countless incidents of miraculous protection have shown. His love through our faith even has power over the forces of nature. As Jesus stilled the tempest, so also can we in His name, when we know that the earth is the Lord's and the fullness thereof, and that He has given us dominion over it.

The energies of love can penetrate even into the earth itself, so that "destructive" earthquakes, even though prophesied, do not destroy, so that obedient winds cleanse the air, so that rain falls comfortingly upon dry places, and rivers of water rise in the desert in answer to man's loving prayers. Even the birds in the desert sing their songs of praise: "Oh all ye fowls of the air, bless ye the Lord: praise Him, and magnify Him forever." The winds, quieted by the love and faith of man, cease from destruction and praise

Him: "Oh ye winds of God, bless ye the Lord: praise Him, and magnify Him forever." The faults below the mountains are quieted by the love of man and praise the Lord: "Oh ye mountains and hills, bless ye the Lord: praise Him, and magnify Him forever."

Even growing things respond, as science has now discovered, to love and prayer, and the earth that languished and lost its fertility when man first sinned against God can bring forth life in a wonderful way when man loves it and prays for it. "Oh all ye green things upon the earth, bless ye the Lord: praise Him, and magnify Him forever."

He commanded us to tell the good news of His love to every creature—to every living thing—that all may in their own ways absorb God's love and, returning joy for joy, give praise to God. As God has dominion over the terrifying and illimitable blackness of inter-stellar space and over every star that evolves there through the aeons, so man by God's decree and by His love through Jesus Christ has dominion over our little earth.

But we are so small, so helpless—how can we do it? Thus the disciples must have felt as they stood gazing into heaven and longing with all their hearts and souls to see Jesus. Then God's messengers said to them, "This same Jesus. . . shall so come in like manner as ye have seen Him go into heaven" (Acts 1: 11). And they remembered His promise and His command, and went to Jerusalem to await His return. For they longed to see Jesus, even as we long to see Him.

"We would see Jesus, for the shadows lengthen
Upon the little landscape of our life."

When His Holy Spirit came upon them they saw Him indeed—not outside themselves but within! And they felt His power entering through the wind and fire but established within them, so that when in His name they sent forth His words, "Arise and walk," the words did not return unto them void, but accomplished their purpose. The very force of His power impelled them out into the world to tell to every creature that Jesus is Lord of all, and that His God, who is our God, is love. They had to go and carry His love everywhere. His love itself compelled them to go.

I wonder whether the disciples still longed to see Him outside of themselves, to look on His face, to behold the light in His eyes and the love in His smile. I am sure they did, for that longing is deep in all of us even when we deny Him, even when we do not know whence comes our dissatisfaction with the world and with life.

I myself, so I am told, first gave expression to this longing when not quite two years old. The incident speaks to me as a parable even now. I was in my mother's arms at a railway station, fleeing from China during the Boxer rebellion. Before that I had never seen nor heard a train, and as it came rushing and roaring into the station I was terrified and cried out, apparently in answer to my mother who must have told me that God would take care of me: "Where *is* God? Baby want to *see* God!"

We still want to see God. And since (finding the ark of the covenant and pillars of cloud and burning bushes inadequate channels for His light) He has shone on us in the face of Jesus Christ, we want to see Jesus. We are terrified of the train of a rushing, roaring life, not knowing that it is going to take us safely home.

It is a long journey in this shrieking, rattling world, but we will see Jesus in the smiles of those who love us, and in the tears of those who need us. We will see Him as His power goes through us to comfort, to save and to heal. We will see Him in the gentleness of flowers, and in the merriment of birds that sing, and in the shy, wild grace of living creatures in the desert. His face will shine on us as the rising sun gilds the mountain-tops, and as rosy day goes quietly to rest. In the thunderous crashing of ocean waves we will feel His power, and in the high wail of the wind from far away.

It is a long journey to paradise, but we will be with Him there as the dying thief was with Him, amid the green pastures and still waters of that prototype of earth. Time stretches forth unbelievably in the heavenly kingdom where in some great mystery we shall go from strength to strength in His perfect service, until the day when, "Every creature which is in heaven, and on the earth, and under the earth, and such as are in the sea, and all that are in them, heard I saying, Blessing, and honour, and glory, and power, be unto him that sitteth upon the throne, and unto the Lamb for ever and ever" (Rev. 5: 13).

Then we shall see Him even as we are seen by Him, not through a glass darkly, but face to face. And who knows how often on that long journey we shall see Him in visions and in dreams, and even standing beside us and smiling on us with His love, as we go into all the world obeying Him? Who knows?

PRAYER

EVEN SO, come Lord Jesus, for we would see you as the shadows lengthen on the little landscape of our life. Even so come, and uphold us by your power, and warm us with your love, that we may go forth and tell to all the world that you are Lord, and that your God and our God is love.

Help us to know that as your love sweetens and enriches the land on which we live, and your wisdom illumines the minds of men, this earth will yet be saved from destruction and become the kingdom of heaven.

Help us to believe that your kingdom really can come, and that your will actually can be done here on earth even as it is in heaven. Open windows to heaven so that we may see its glory re-created upon the earth, and thus draw that kingdom toward us by our holy seeing. Stir up our imaginations that we may vision this earth as you, Lord God, created or desire it to be. Perhaps we may imagine a man from the dead moon, or arid Mars, or clouded Venus, looking on the earth with its green fields and rushing rivers, its glimmering peaks and painted deserts, all clothed in myriads of shining flowers. Surely such a man would sigh, "It is heaven!"

And it *is* heaven. It needs only to be nourished and permeated with your love, oh Lord, so that all the potential beauty in man and animal, in earth and sea, may blossom and bring forth the fruit of righteousness, and all evil sown by the enemy be crowded out and seen no more. So let your light shine upon it, dear Lord, that it may in the unimaginable vistas of eternity merge into the many-dimensional way of life that is immortality and the heaven of heavens, Amen.